GW00482803

THE
Early Years

To _____

From _____

First published in Great Britain in 2002 by
Azure
1 Marylebone Road
London NW1 4DU

Published in the United States in 2003 by
Paraclete Press
Brewster, Massachusetts
www.paracletepress.com
ISBN 1-55725-302-1

Copyright © Pat Wynnejones 2002

All rights reserved. No part of this book may be reproduced
or transmitted in any form or by any means, electronic or
mechanical, including photocopying, recording, or by any
information storage and retrieval system, without permission
in writing from the publisher.

British Library Cataloguing-in-Publication Data

A catalogue record for this book is available from the
British Library

ISBN 1-902694-23-6

Designed by Mary Gorton
Printed in Singapore

To Harriet, my dear daughter-in-law

THE
Early Years

AN ILLUSTRATED ANTHOLOGY
Compiled by Pat Wynnejones

A New Baby

O baby, baby, baby dear
We lie alone together here;
The snowy gown and cap and sheet
With lavender are fresh and sweet;
Through half-closed blinds the roses peer
To see and love you, baby dear.

We are so tired, we like to lie
Just doing nothing, you and I,
Within the darkened room,
The sun sends dusk rays through the gloom
Which is no gloom since you are here.
My little life, my baby dear.

EDITH NESBIT BLAND

The First Born FREDERICK WILLIAM ELWELL

'Soft, sleepy mouth...'

Soft, sleepy mouth so vaguely pressed
Against your new-made mother's breast,
Soft little hands in mine I fold,
Soft little feet I kiss and hold,
Round, soft, smooth head and tiny ear
All mine, my own, my baby dear.

EDITH NESBIT

Mother and Child NORMAN HEPPLE

Baptism

Little baby on my arm,
tiny, tender and frail,
God keep you ever from all harm,
so that no evil may assail
you. Today you become a prince
of Light. Baptismal waters will rinse
out every trace
of our First Parents' disgrace.
You'll be dressed in purest
white – sacramental grace.
Angels shall rejoice at the
sight and kiss you.

MARY FRANCES MOONEY

Maternity HENRI LEBASQUE

The Maker of Cradles

He makes little cradles of fine lacquered wood,
He paints them with dragons and stars and birds,
They are carven and coloured and lined with silk,
And he weaves a charm for them to woven words.

('Where shall I rest your little tired head?
Son of my heart, lie still,' she said.)

He makes little cradles of beaten bronze;
As light as a leaf is the fretted screen;
The pillow is scented with jasmin flowers,
The silken blanket is fit for a queen.

('Where shall I rest your little tired head?
Son of my heart, lie still,' she said.)

He makes little cradles of silver and gold,
Silver and ivory gem the hood,
They swing from a peacock's outspread tail,
And the rockers are carved of sandal-wood.

('Where shall I rest your little tired head?
Son of my heart, lie still,' she said.)

The gipsy mother goes humbly by,
The babe in her arms lies warm and still,
Oh! Maker of Cradles, you cannot weave
A lovelier cradle, for all your skill.

('Where shall I rest your little tired head?
Son of my heart, lie still,' she said.)

THORA STOWELL

Motherhood LOUIS (EMILE) ADAN

Child Asleep

Soft, in silent slumber there he lies,
the night cascading round him like a veil;
restoring sleep in those refreshing eyes
and draped around his snowy limbs, as pale
as one who lies in death's long sleep.

The stillness of the night goes undisturbed
by that deep rise and falling of his breast,
as cool the tides of breath flow unperturbed
in gentle sleep. There in his hand, tight-pressed,
a rosary of tiny beads

Is held as gently as the night holds stars.
And every deep and reverential sigh
holds whispered dreams so far removed from ours,
in worlds in which the angels learn to fly,
but we can't reach for all our words.

I, too, could pray in dreams so long ago,
but now I search for peace in children's eyes,
to find the way to what I used to know
before I grew too serious and wise
to understand their innocence.

I pray that I could pray as children pray,
without the need for argument and words;
then rise as children rise at break of day,
knowing that the children's King has heard,
and laughs with them in heaven every hour.

CHRISTINA M. CROFT

The Three Sisters JOHANN GEORG MEYER VON BREMEN

Child Waking

The child sleeps in the daytime,
With his abandoned, with his jetsam look,
On the bare mattress, across the cot's corner;
Covers and toys thrown out, a routine labour.

Relaxed in sleep and light,
Face upwards, never so clear a prey to eyes;
Like a walled town, surprised out of the air
– All life called in, yet all laid bare

To the enemy above –
He has taken cover in daylight, gone to ground
In his own short length, his body strong in bleached
Blue cotton and his arms outstretched.

Now he opens his eyes but not
To see at first; they reflect the light like snow
And I wait in doubt if he sleeps or wakes, till I see
Slight pain of effort at the boundary,

And hear how the trifling wound
Of bewilderment fetches a caverned cry
As he crosses out of sleep – at once to recover
His place and poise, and smile as I lift him over.

But I recall the blue-
white snowfield of his eyes empty of sight
High between dream and day, and think how there
The soul might rise visible as a flower.

EDITH J. SCOVELL

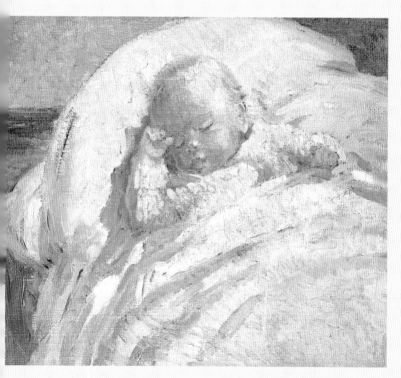

A Sleeping Baby DOROTHEA SHARP

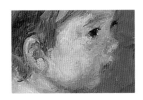

The First Tooth

Through the house what busy joy,
Just because the infant boy
Has a tiny tooth to show!
I have got a double row,
All as white and all as small;
Yet no one cares for mine at all.
He can say but half a word,
Yet that single sound's preferred
To all the words that I can say
In the longest summer day.
He cannot walk, yet if he put
With mimic motion out his foot,
As if he were advancing
It's more prized than my best dancing.

CHARLES AND MARY LAMB

Woman and Children MARY CASSATT

Ellen Learning to Walk

My beautiful trembler! how wildly she shrinks!
     And how wistful she looks while she lingers!
Papa is extremely uncivil, she thinks,
     She but pleaded for one of his fingers!

What eloquent pleading! the hand stretching out,
     As if doubting so strange a refusal;
While her blue eyes say plainly, 'What is he about
     That he does not assist me as usual?!'

Come on, my pet Ellen! we won't let you slip –
     Unclasp those soft arms from his knee, love;
I see a faint smile round that exquisite lip,
     A smile half reproach and half glee, love.

So! that's my brave baby! one foot falters forward,
     Half doubtful the other steals by it!
What, shrinking, again! why, you shy little coward!
     'Twon't kill you to walk a bit! – try it!

There! steady, my darling! huzza! I have caught her!
     I clasp her, caress'd and caressing!
She hides her bright face, as if what we have taught her
     Were something to hide for – the blessing!

Now back again! Bravo! that shout of delight,
     How it thrills to the hearts that adore her!
Joy, joy for her mother! and blest be the night
     When her little light feet first upbore her!

FRANCES SARGENT OSGOOD

The First Steps JEAN-FRANCOIS MILLET

A Lullaby

Lullee, lullay,
I could not love thee more
If thou wast Christ the King.
Now tell me, how did Mary know
That in her womb should sleep and grow
The Lord of everything?

Lullee, lullay,
An angel stood with her
Who said, 'That which doth stir
Like summer in thy side
Shall save the world from sin.
Then stable, hall and inn
Shall cherish Christmas-tide.'

Lullee, lullay,
And so it was that day.
And did she love him more
Because an angel came
To prophesy his name?
Ah no, not so,
She could not love him more,
But loved him just the same.
Lullee, lullee, lullay.

JANET LEWIS

The Eleventh Hour, the Eleventh Day of the Eleventh Month   W. PERCY DAY

First Birthday

One candle on a cake,
One year of happy days –
That was your gift to me,
Watching your baby ways.

One candle on a cake,
How fast those days have fled!
But I'll be loving you
All through the days ahead.

PAT WYNNEJONES

One Year Old HELEN ALLINGHAM

Having our Tea

There's something religious in the way we sit
At the tea table, a tidy family of three.
You, my love, slicing the bread and butter, and she,
The red-cheeked tot a smear of blackberry jam, and me...
A new creation is established, a true presence.
And talking to each other, breaking words over food
Is somehow different from customary chatting.

BOBI JONES

Family Portrait VICTOR MIKOLAYOVICH

'Lord, we thank thee...'

Lord, we thank thee for our children
    With their faces bright and fair,
With their laughter and their temper,
    Waking gladness, bringing care:
Teach us how to keep them upright,
    True and gallant, everywhere.

W. CHARTER PIGGOTT

Portraits of Children, or *The Children of Martial Caillebotte* PIERRE AUGUSTE RENOIR

The Land of Story-Books

At evening when the lamp is lit,
Around the fire my parents sit;
They sit at home and talk and sing,
And do not play at anything.

Now, with my little gun, I crawl
All in the dark along the wall,
And follow round the forest track
Away behind the sofa back.

There, in the night, where none can spy,
All in my hunter's camp I lie,
And play at books that I have read
Till it is time to go to bed.

ROBERT LOUIS STEVENSON

After the Battle ANGUS MacDONALL

'When a child...'

When a child walks down the road,
a company of angels goes before him proclaiming,
'Make way for
the image of the Holy One'.

JOHANN CHRISTOPH ARNOLD

At the Edge of the Wood KEN MARONEY

Thanksgiving Day

Over the river and through the wood,
To grandfather's house we go;
    The horse knows the way
    To carry the sleigh
Through the white and drifted snow.

Over the river and through the wood –
Oh, how the wind does blow!
    It stings the toes
    And bites the nose,
As over the ground we go.

Over the river and through the wood,
To have a first-rate play.
    To hear bells ring,
    'Ting-a-ling-ding!'
Hurrah for Thanksgiving Day!

Over the river and through the wood,
Trot fast, my dapple-grey!
    Spring over the ground,
    Like a hunting hound!
For this is Thanksgiving Day.

Over the river and through the wood,
And straight through the barnyard gate,
   We seem to go
   Extremely slow –
It is so hard to wait!

Over the river and through the wood –
Now grandmother's cap I spy!
   Hurrah for the fun!
   Is the pudding done?
Hurrah for the pumpkin-pie!

L. MARIA CHILD

The Horse Sleigh VINCENT HADDELSEY

Childhood Reds

The laughing reds that children love, toy wagon wheels and tops,
The firecrackers' sudden red and sticky lollipops,
Balloons that tug impatiently against restraining ties,
The hearts of lacy Valentines, the dribbled juice of pies,
Red mittens, natty robin's breasts, and circus lemonade,
A fire-engine's splendour in a holiday parade.
The healthy glow of frost-nipped cheeks, chapped knuckles,
knees and ears,
A rabbit's eyes, the holly's red when Santa Claus appears.
A dove's quick feet, a puppy's tongue, the patterns in a rug,
A turkey's neck, a baby's toes, a spotted lady-bug,
Red felt that binds a grubby slate, red bird-kites in the breeze,
And all the gay exciting reds of festive Christmas trees.

DON BLANDING

Santa Claus Scattering Presents DAVID COOKE

'Many things can wait...'

Many things can wait. Children cannot.
Today their bones are being formed, their blood
is being made, their senses are being developed.
To them we cannot say 'tomorrow'.
Their name is today.

GABRIELA MISTRAL

The Young Cricketer EDITH HAYLLAR

The Little Green Orchard

Some one is always sitting there,
      In the little green orchard;
  Even when the sun is high,
  In noon's unclouded sky,
  And faintly droning goes
  The bee from rose to rose,
Some one in shadow is sitting there,
      In the little green orchard.

Yes, and when twilight's falling softly
      On the little green orchard;
  When the grey dew distils
  And every flower-cup fills;
  When the last blackbird says,
  'What – what!' and goes her way – ssh!
I have heard voices calling softly
      In the little green orchard.

WALTER DE LA MARE

In the Orchard EDWARD ATKINSON HORNEL

'We could never...'

We could never
have loved the earth so well
if we'd had no childhood in it.

GEORGE ELIOT

Footballers, Kos ANDREW MACARA

The Boy's Song

Where the pools are bright and deep,
Where the grey trout lies asleep,
Up the river and o'er the lea –
That's the way for Billy and me.

Where the blackbird sings the latest,
Where the hawthorn blooms the sweetest,
Where the nestlings chirp and flee –
That's the way for Billy and me.

Where the mowers mow the cleanest,
Where the hay lies thick and greenest,
There to trace the homeward bee –
That's the way for Billy and me.

There let us walk, there let us play,
Through the meadows, among the hay,
Up the water, and o'er the lea –
That's the way for Billy and me.

JAMES HOGG

Children with their Dog, Bois de Boulogne Lake, Paris MAX AGOSTINI

A Wish for my Children

On this doorstep I stand
year after year
and watch you leaving

and think: May you not
skin your knees. May you
not catch your fingers
in car doors. May
your hearts not break.

May tide and weather
wait for your coming

and may you grow strong
to break
all webs of my weaving.

EVANGELINE PATERSON

Maternal Love VICENZO IROLLI

Acknowledgements

The publishers acknowledge with thanks permission to reproduce the material listed below:

A NEW BABY by Edith Nesbit Bland
Illustration: **The First Born**, 1913 by Frederick William Elwell (1870–1958)
Ferens Art Gallery, Hull City Museums and Art Galleries, UK. Courtesy of the artist's estate/Bridgeman Art Library

'SOFT SLEEPY MOUTH…' by Edith Nesbit
Illustration: **Mother and Child** by Norman Hepple (1908–94)
The Potteries Museum and Art Gallery, Stoke-on-Trent, UK/Bridgeman Art Library

BAPTISM by Mary Frances Monney, from The Poetry Church, published by Feather Books
Illustration: **Maternity** by Henri Lebasque (1865–1937)
Noortman, Maastricht, Netherlands/ Bridgeman Art Library

THE MAKER OF CRADLES by Thora Stowell, from The Voice of Youth, published by The Poetry Society, Summer 1957
Illustration: **Motherhood**, 1898 by Louis (Emile) Adan (1839–1937)
Waterhouse and Dodd, London, UK/ Bridgeman Art Library

CHILD ASLEEP by Christina M. Croft, from The Poetry Church, published by Feather Books
Illustration: **The Three Sisters** by Johann Georg Meyer von Bremen (1813–86)
Josef Mensing Gallery, Hamm-Rhynern, Germany/Bridgeman Art Library

CHILD WAKING by Edith J. Scovell, from The Penguin Book of Contemporary Verse, ed. K. Allott

Illustration: **A Sleeping Baby** by Dorothy Sharp (1874–1955)
Private Collection/Bonhams, London, UK Bridgeman Art Library

THE FIRST TOOTH by Charles and Mary Lamb
Illustration: **Woman and Children**, 1906 by Mary Cassatt (1844–1926)
Fogg Art Museum, Harvard University Art Museums, USA/Bridgeman Art Library

ELLEN LEARNING TO WALK by Frances Sargent Osgood
Illustration: **The First Steps** by Jean-Francois Millet (1814–75)
Bibliotheque Nationale, Paris/Bridgeman Art Library

A LULLABY by Janet Lewis, from The Lion Book of Christian Poetry
Illustration: **The Eleventh Hour, the Eleventh Day of the Eleventh Month**, 1918, 1919 by W. Percy Day (fl.1905–22)
Harris Museum and Art Gallery, Preston, Lancashire, UK/Bridgeman Art Library

FIRST BIRTHDAY by Pat Wynnejones
Illustration: **One Year Old** by Helen Allingham (1848–1926)
John Noott Galleries, Broadway, Worcestershire, UK/Bridgeman Art Library

HAVING OUR TEA by Bobi Jones, originally in Welsh, translated by Joseph B Clancy, twentieth century, from The Lion Book of Christian Poetry.
Illustration: **Family Portrait** by Victor Mikolayovich (fl. 1956)
Bonhams, London, UK/Bridgeman Art Library

RD, WE THANK THEE...' words
W. Charter Piggott (1872–1943) from
arged Songs of Praise, 1931, Oxford
iversity Press

Istration: **Portraits of Children, or The
Children of Martial Caillebotte**, 1895 by
rre Auguste Renoir (1841–1919)
vate Collection/Bridgeman Art Library

IE LAND OF STORY-BOOKS by
bert Louis Stevenson

istration: **After the Battle** by Angus
cDonall (b. 1876)
rbes Magazine Collection, New York,
SA/Bridgeman Art Library

VHEN A CHILD WALKS...' by
hann Christoph Arnold, taken with
rmission from Endangered © 2000 by
ough Publishing House

istration: **At the Edge of the Wood**, Ken
aroney (contemporary artist)
onhams, London, UK/Bridgeman Art
brary

HANKSGIVING DAY by L. Maria
hild

lustration: **The Horse Sleigh** by Vincent
laddelsey (contemporary artist)
rivate Collection/Bridgeman Art Library

CHILDHOOD REDS by Don Blanding,
om A Desk Drawer Anthology, compiled
y Alice Roosevelt Longworth and
heodore Roosevelt, published by
lutchison. 'Childhood Reds' appeared in
Memory Room, published by Dodd, Mead
nd Company Inc.

lustration: **Santa Claus Scattering Presents**
by David Cooke (contemporary artist)
Private Collection/Bridgeman Art Library

'MANY THINGS CAN WAIT...' by
Gabriela Mistral

Illustration: **The Young Cricketer**, 1904
by Edith Hayllar (1860–1948)
Private Collection. Courtesy of the artist's
estate/Bridgeman Art Library

THE LITTLE GREEN ORCHARD by
Walter de la Mare, from The Complete
Poems of Walter de la Mare, 1969, by
permission of The Literary Trustees of
Walter de la Mare and the Society of
Authors as their representative.

Illustration: **In the Orchard** by Edward
Atkinson Hornel (1864–1933)
City of Edinburgh Museums and Art
Galleries, Scotland/Bridgeman Art Library

'WE COULD NEVER...' by George
Eliot, from The Mill on the Floss

Illustration: **Footballers, Kos**, 1993 by
Andrew Macara (contemporary artist)
Private Collection/Bridgeman Art Library

THE BOY'S SONG by James Hogg

Illustration: **Children with their Dog,
Bois de Boulogne Lake, Paris** by
Max Agostini (1914–97)
Galerie Martin-Caille Matignon, Paris,
France/Bridgeman Art Library

A WISH FOR MY CHILDREN by
Evangeline Paterson

Illustration: **Maternal Love** by Vicenzo
Irolli (1860–1942)
Josef Mensing Gallery, Hamm-Rhynern,
Germany/Bridgeman Art Library

Every effort has been made to trace and acknowledge
copyright holders of material reproduced in this
book. We apologize for any errors or omissions and
would ask those concerned to contact the publishers.